SRA
OPEN COURT READING

At the Farm

A Division of The **McGraw·Hill** *Companies*

Columbus, Ohio

www.sra4kids.com

SRA/McGraw-Hill

*A Division of The **McGraw·Hill** Companies*

Send all inquiries to:
SRA/McGraw-Hill
8787 Orion Place
Columbus, OH 43240-4027

ISBN 0-07-569475-1
   3 4 5 6 7 8 9 DBH 05 04 03 02

"Mom, what was it like on a farm?"
Darla asked.
"I had hard jobs. I had to start after
the alarm buzzed. I did my part."

"I helped Dad plant a garden, Darla.
I planted corn and parsnips."

"I helped Mom with the chickens.
I got the eggs."

"Then I helped in the barn."

"I had fun, too, Darla. I got to help make fudge. Mmmmm! Such rich fudge. It was fun."

"This is Gran and Gramps's farm, Darla.
You can help on the farm on this trip."